Michael Frei

How Important are Education, Human Capital and Knowledge for Economic Growth and Development?

How have these factors been incorporated into endogenous growth models?

GRIN Verlag

Bibliografische Information der Deutschen Nationalbibliothek:

Die Deutsche Bibliothek verzeichnet diese Publikation in der Deutschen National-
bibliografie; detaillierte bibliografische Daten sind im Internet über http://dnb.d-
nb.de/ abrufbar.

Imprint:

Copyright © 2009 GRIN Verlag GmbH
Druck und Bindung: Books on Demand GmbH, Norderstedt Germany
ISBN: 978-3-656-47242-1

This book at GRIN:

http://www.grin.com/en/e-book/230774/how-important-are-education-human-
capital-and-knowledge-for-economic-growth

GRIN - Your knowledge has value

Der GRIN Verlag publiziert seit 1998 wissenschaftliche Arbeiten von Studenten, Hochschullehrern und anderen Akademikern als eBook und gedrucktes Buch. Die Verlagswebsite www.grin.com ist die ideale Plattform zur Veröffentlichung von Hausarbeiten, Abschlussarbeiten, wissenschaftlichen Aufsätzen, Dissertationen und Fachbüchern.

Visit us on the internet:

http://www.grin.com/

http://www.facebook.com/grincom

http://www.twitter.com/grin_com

How important are education, human capital and knowledge for economic growth and development?

How have these factors been incorporated into endogenous growth models? Discuss their relevance

By Michael Frei
for the course in "Development economics"
Summer Semester 2009
Free University of Bozen/Bolzano

Introduction

In his speech at the Inaugural Convention of the African Federation of Human Resource Management Association in Botswana, Professor David Abulai (2008) stated that quality and quantity of human capital is becoming increasingly evident for the economic development of nations in today's knowledge era. In fact the world of today is influenced by steady technological and scientific progress; by means of these new developments the socio-economic conditions in which people live are increasingly improving. Nevertheless a big part of the world is still lagging behind and social and economic distinctions still exist and developing countries are trying to catch up. Professor Abulai (2008) argued that the key to this catching up in development is the population itself, which has to be educated, healthy and qualified in order to deal with new scientific and technological inventions and to exploit this new opportunities in the best possible way. The aim of this paper will be in the first part to analyze the impact of education, human capital and knowledge for economic growth and development. In the second part of this paper the incorporation of human capital into endogenous growth models will be examined, focusing on the two main branches of growth analysis pioneered by Romer (1990) and Lucas (1988).

The effect on growth

Considering the definition of the OECD (2001), the human capital of a nation consists of all knowledge, skills, and competencies, embodied in every individual citizen, that facilitate the creation of personal, social and economic well-being. Taking into consideration this definition, it is very difficult to find a way how to measure the influence of human capital on national economies adequately. One of the main problems in the measurement of human capital is the difficulty to measure its quality, because it is not traded in markets like other economic goods and therefore no clear market value can be assigned to it. In statistics and empirical studies, researchers have to refer on educational attainments, literacy rate and enrolment rates to assign a value to the quality level of human capital of a state (Coloumbe, 2004).

Domenech (2002) states that, according to his empirical studies, literacy rate results to be the best indicator of the quality of human capital. In OECD countries literacy rate has proven to be a better indicator than inscription- and attendance rates in educational institutions. Domenech found a strong positive relationship between literacy rate and long-run economic growth and productivity; this result contradicts to the prior study of Islam (1995) who claims that in OECD countries no significant connection between human capital, education and growth can be found. But Domenech argues, that the effect of education which is significant for growth, can be found mainly in the educational level of the general labor force, the significance of top-level education for economic growth is only marginal or not existing. A reason for this finding could be the globalization and therewith the high mobility and willingness to transfer of high-educated labor forces.

Another important finding of Domenech's studies is the impact of female labor-market-participation, literacy- and fertility rate on economic growth. Domenech states that female literacy rate and participation in the labor market has a stronger positive relationship to economic growth than the literacy- and participation rate of men. But this finding can also be explained by taking into consideration, that in countries with high economic growth in general women are more likely to participate in the labor market and get increasing possibilities to enjoy education, because social barriers to women education are disappearing in high-developed countries. Therefore growth can also be the activator of higher female educational and literacy level and not vice versa. However it is commonly agreed that female participation rate is one of the key factor in measuring the development of a country.

Coloumbe (2004) argues that in further studies on the impact of human capital on the development of countries, human capital should be measured directly by literacy tests and scores and not indirectly by years of schooling. According to different empirical studies, it can be seen very clearly that years of schooling have no significant relationship with growth while international comparable literacy and test scores have a positive impact on it, so Canada. Therefore it can be concluded that human capital and education matter to the well-being of developing nations if measured by qualitative standards. However in a recent study the OECD (2006) states that one additional educational year could increase the productivity and GDP of a nation between three and 6 per cent.

There are three main reasons why human capital has a great importance on developing economies. Firstly human capital increases the innovative capacities of companies and economies; this is mainly important for self-sustained growth. Secondly a skilled labor force is able to capitalize opportunities created by globalization and imported technology; that means it provides the skill levels for workers to adapt successfully to new challenges. Thirdly human capital creates the fundamental conditions for technological advancement. To sum up, knowledge, education and human capital are essential factors for economic development of nations.

Incorporation into endogenous growth models

In contrary to the basic Sollow model, in which long-run economic growth is treated as an exogenous factor, endogenous growth models try to explain economic growth as caused within the model. The main problem of endogenising economic growth into a model is lack of a coherent social science perspective and the difficulty to interpret the regressions based on endogenous models. Furthermore in the new growth models it gets hard to distinguish between different theories (Leeuwen, 2006).

In the sector of development economics the two most important branches in endogenous growth theory are the Lucas (1988) and the Romer (1990) model. Lucas (1988) sees human capital as the sum of skills that are part of physical persons, as individual skills they are naturally excludable and partly rival. On the other hand Romer (1990) defines human capital as ideas and knowledge which are shared by the whole society and therefore are not rival and only to some extent excludable. Considering this differences, Romer (1990), in his model, implements human capital as an input in the sector of research and development, while Lucas (1988) implements it as a factor of production, like capital or labor.

Following this argumentation, in theory the Lucasian model creates endogenous growth by increasing human-capital while on the other hand marginal returns do not decrease. The Romarian model is build up on the accumulation of technology and knowledge and therefore the economy grows if technological advancement is made or new knowledge is gained. So in the Romarian model growth can happen even if returns of scale of investment in human capital are negative, because it is not a factor of production but causes technological advancement which result in an increase in GDP without increasing human capital.

Leeuwen (2006) found that for most countries the Lucasian model explains the effect of human capital on growth correctly, but he states that on the other hand there are also examples (i.e. Japan) where growth happened even if the marginal returns of human capital investments were decreasing. By testing the two theories in a sample country using regression analysis, it can be found which one is right in that particular situation. If the human capital level has a significant positive influence on the growth of an economy, than human capital works as originator of technological advancement and therewith the Romer (1990) model is proves to be correct. But if the per capita level of human capital increases and in consequence causes economic growth, than Lucas (1988) is right, because than the personal skills which are rival and excludable cause growth. Leeuwen (2006) shows this process mathematically with the following formula:

$$\Delta Lny_t = \alpha + kt + \beta_1 \Delta Lny_{t-1} + \beta_2 Lny_{t-1} + \beta_3 \ln hc_{t-1} + \beta_4 \Delta \ln hc_{t-1} + \varepsilon \quad (1)$$

In this equation y denotes the GDP per capita, t the starting year and hc the stock of human capital per capita. It can be seen in this formula that, for example if $ß_3$ increases significantly and positive than Romer's (1990) theory of human capital as technology fertilisator is fulfilled, on the other hand if $ß_4$ causes economic growth than Lucas (1988) keeps right.

By using this equation on different countries, Leeuwen (2006) found that results are differing from country to country, while the majority of the tested Asian countries experienced Lucasian growth, other ones (esp. Japan) experienced Romarian growth. As soon as Japan experienced diminishing returns to scale on human capital investments it moved towards Romarian growth, while in other countries like for example in Indonesia this didn't happen, even if returns of scale began to diminish there too. For Japan the shift from Lucasian to Romarian growth can be explained by the better educational system in Japan and the strong connection between its educational system and economy.

This is a very good example because it shows the difficulty of the implementation of human capital, education and knowledge into growth models, it is a very complex issue to interpret the regression based on these endogenous growth models and therefore it is not possible to get accurate results. Nevertheless by the implementation it can be seen that empirical studies show that a significant positive relationship between human capital and growth exists.

Conclusion

To sum up it is commonly agreed, that human capital is an important factor for growth whereas the significance of the relationship is not clear because of a big degree of variation in the results of empirical studies. In order to get comparable results unified methods of measurement of human capital and education should be used worldwide; therewith standardized data could be collected. But even with standardized data it rests difficult to compare different countries because the economic and social structures differ and therefore this data can't be considered equal. Nevertheless universal factors like gender ratio and literacy offer a good basis to analyze the relationship between human capital, knowledge, education and economic growth.

Considering the implementation of human capital into endogenous growth models, the same difficulties like described in the first paragraph of this conclusion make it hard to make clear statements about the relationship of human capital and economic growth. But it is a fact that the Lucas (1988) model works for most developing countries, while the Romarian model works only for exceptional cases. But it should be kept in mind that also the framework of Romer (1990) includes some important factors that have to be included in the development economics branch especially in endogenous growth theory.

We can conclude from the analysis in this paper that human capital is a very important factor in understanding the economies of developing countries. When economic policies are implemented especially in LDC's and LMDC's, governments have to consider that human capital, knowledge and education make part of the key factors to sustained economic growth and therewith to catch up to higher developed countries. Institutions have to keep in mind that to achieve the millennium goals set up by the UN, which aim to end poverty by the year 2015 education, it is necessary to focus on the education of people and the formation of a strong basis of human capital in poor and developing countries.

Bibliography

Abulai, D.(2008). *Human capital and innovation*. Retrived March 8, 2009, from UNISA Website: http://www.sblunisa.ac.za/content.php?section=28&article=331

Coloumbe, Serge (2004), "International Adult Literacy Survey: Literacy scores, human capital and growth across fourteen OECD countries", Statistics Canada Department of Economics, University of Ottawa.

Doménech, R. (2002), "Human capital in growth regressions: How much difference does data quality make?". *Manuscript. Instituto de Análisis Económico (CSIC) and Universidad de Valencia.*

Islam, N. (1995). "Growth empirics: A panel data approach". *The Quarterly Journal of Economics,* Vol. 110.

Leeuwen, Bas van (2006). "The role of human capital in endogenous growth in India, Indonesia and Japan", XIV International Economic History Congress, Helsinki.

Lucas, Robert (1988), "On the Mechanics of Economic Development", *Journal of Monetary Economics,* Vol. 22.

OECD (2001), *The Well-being of Nations: The Role of Human and Social Capital,* OECD publication, Paris.

Romer, Paul. (1990), "Endogenous Technological Change", *Journal of Political Economy,* Vol. 98.